Talk English

The Secret To Speak English Like A Native In 6 Months For Busy People, Learn Spoken English From The Success

Ken Xiao

ISBN-10:0-9981632-0-1
ISBN-13:978-0-9981632-0-8

DEDICATION

This book is dedicated to my wife, Mei. Thank you for your positive energy throughout our life journey. Thank you.

THIS is the book every English learner NEEDS to read.
Crystal F. , Canada

After 2 weeks, the change is significant. Most importantly I think like a native speaker starting building a little bit in my subconsciousness.
Dexuan L., China

How I can speak English so fast without accent? With your tips I can do it. I will recommend to my friends with broken English because I think your book is very helpful for me and other people like me to learn speak fluent English. Thank you so much!
Farah A., Iran

The book provides the readers a workable way on how to get to speak fluent English. It's simple, straightforward, and most important of all, its focused and not too way long to cost the readers too much time.
Joanne L., Hong Kong

I like your book especially all of your suggestions how to improve the English and soften the accent. Thanks!
Kasia L., Poland

There are so many books , specifically "help" books, out on the market that one can get so overwhelmed with the selection. This book, catering to the English language fluency, is such a great book that there is no need to even scratch your head over the others.
Leona Y., Czech Republic

Download your free audio and video in Lesson 1.

Editor's Word

Before having read the book, my expectations of its effectiveness were neutral-- I wasn't sure if the 6-month plan that would be set forth by the author would be a realistic timeline for an individual's learning needs. Regardless, I dove in with a completely open mind and almost immediately came to realize that my doubts were unfounded.

The book's main promise was that it would provide its readers with a plan that would transform their broken English into fluent English. After having read this piece, I can say without a doubt that the book went above and beyond its initial promise to deliver SO much more. Ken outlined a meticulously detailed regimen that not only explained everything one would have to do in order to improve his or her English (including numerous original strategies and helpful tips) but he also took on the role of an encourager, cheering his reader on throughout the whole read. Certainly, this book went above and beyond to deliver much more than its original promise—it delivered a lifestyle change.

The strategies that the author has outlined can be applied universally to any language and I would recommend this book to anyone who would like to improve his or her fluency in a foreign language (most specifically English as this is what the author focuses on). THIS is the book every English learner NEEDS to read. What sets this book apart from the myriad of others is the way in which the author connects with his reader; from his words, you can absolutely feel the suffering he experienced as result of his broken English and the triumph that overwhelmed him when he finally succeeded at communicating fluently. This book is thoughtful and inspiring and its genuine tone will deeply touch its readers.

Crystal Faqiri

Foreword

There are so many books , specifically "help" books, out on the market that one can get so overwhelmed with the selection. This book, catering to the English language fluency, is such a great book that there is no need to even scratch your head over the others. Ken does an incredible job at making it easy to read and understand, precise and specific in teaching you what to do to better your English, and most important, he makes it personal. With the personal touch, you can really fall deep into the emotions, the battles and the triumphs of Ken's journey. He takes you into a place where you can really relate to him and that makes learning so much easier...and more fun!

I, myself, am not an American Native. I was born in the Czech Republic and came to the USA at the age of 4 with my parents. Now as a young child, I picked up the English language quite fast, however my parents did not. As adults, of course, it's much more difficult to learn a second language, let alone English, which is not that easy! They took English as a second language courses at a local community college and watched "easy to understand" TV shows, which was all fine and helped them learn the language, but if they had Ken's book at that time, back in the 1980's, they really would have scored!

Ken is eager and excited to get this book in your hands. He trusts that his tips and techniques will help you, just as they did him! I believe that you will find this book extremely valuable and helpful and hope you enjoy it as much as I did!

Leona Young

About The Author

Ken Xiao

- International #1 best-selling author of English fluency books
- Passionate English teacher with self-help English learning experience who has walked in your shoes before and started to speak English like a native speaker just six months later
- School principal
- Translator, United States Department Of Defense
- Business owner
- Bachelor of Science, Information Technology
- Master of Science, Space Studies
- Creator, MyFluentEnglish Formula
- Author, Talk English: The Secret To Speak English Like A Native In 6 Months For Busy People
- Author, English: Learn To Speak 80% Of Daily English Like A Native In 1 Lesson
- Author, English Pronunciation: Pronounce English Words Like A Pro In 6 Months

10

Table of Contents

You must do the thing you think you cannot do.
Eleanor Roosevelt

Introduction

You have studied English for years, yet you still don't speak English well. You have tried many methods and you still make grammar mistakes, you still can't speak English fluently, and you still can't pronounce English words correctly. You can read, but you feel nervous to speak English or too shy to speak English.

The good news is, this is very normal. You have simply used ineffective methods to learn to speak English.

My name is Ken Xiao. I was in your situation before, but now I can speak English like a native, and I accomplished that in six months without spending a dime. I'm going to teach you how to completely get rid of your accent and develop an American or British accent to speak English just like a native speaker, and I'll teach you how to accomplish that in just six months.

In this book, you'll learn:

* How to speak like a native in six months or less
* How to do that effortlessly on a busy schedule
* How to speak English without translating it first
* How to learn grammar without memorizing grammar rules
* How to build a vocabulary that lasts
* How to make you pronounce English words like native American or native British
* How to speak English fluently, correctly, and naturally just like a native
* And more... to make you speak English like a native speaker.

You have studied English for years, yet you still can't speak English well. The reason is simple: The methods you used were ineffective. Change your way of learning now.

Learn from a successful person who was in your situation before and is getting the result you want. You can succeed by simply doing what I have done before. Effortlessly follow the step-by-step instructions in the book to achieve the highest level of fluency to make you speak English like a native speaker.

Man is not the creature of circumstances, circumstances are the creatures of men. We are free agents, and man is more powerful than matter.
Benjamin Disraeli

1 — A Middle School Dropout Can. Can You? (Must read)

In a poor farming village, a child was born. In his childhood life, he was hungry. So hungry that even after over 30 years, he still remembers the hunger he'd been through in vivid details. There was no running water, so he had to carry water home from a well that was half of a kilometer away using two buckets. He was seven years old. The buckets of water were so heavy that he couldn't walk straight. At age 7, he started to work in the fields to plant, cultivate, and harvest crops. At age 7, he started to collect firewood for cooking. At age 7, he started to cook for the entire family using an open fire. There was no electric stove, and he was lucky if he got electricity for lighting once a week. He started elementary school at age 8 and dropped out of middle school at age 13.

He moved to America with his family when he was 17. He spoke no English, went straight to high school, and started to learn English in classes called English as Second Language (ESL) classes. Since he spoke no English, English certainly wasn't his favorite subject. At age 20, he could speak some broken English. Then he used a method which I'm about to share with you to improve his English fluency, and six months later, he turned his broken English into fluent English. In the following effortless practices, he even turned his English into an English that people who didn't know him thought it was his native language.

Amazing, isn't it?

And here is the best part: This country boy, this middle school dropout, started at 20, for six months, who successfully spoke English like a native, has NO special talent! He's just an average person you and I

17

would see in the country side. He's just an average person you and I would meet on the streets.

This middle school dropout is talking right in front of you. This middle school dropout is me.

And yes, I, Ken Xiao, a country boy, a middle school dropout, an average man, started at 20, for six months, can speak English like a native!

There is one sole purpose I'm putting my humble background here – inspiration! Because with a background like that and I can still make me speak English like a native. Can you?

What I used to make me speak English like a native was MyFluentEnglish Formula. It's a formula I created, improved, and perfected. Using the same formula, I also made me speak two other languages like a native.

If a country boy, a middle school dropout, an average man with no special talent, started at age 20, for six months, can make him speak English like a native, my friend, yes, you can. Let's start the six-month journey today to get your results.

To your success,
Ken Xiao

First family picture taken in 1983. I'm the boy standing in the back.

2 — From Broken English to Fluent English

When I was 20, I could understand some English but not much. My vocabulary was very limited, my accent was very strong, and I first thought in my language, and then translated into my own version of English to speak to people. The problem was, people couldn't understand me.

In short, my English was bad.

New York City. I spoke no English when I came to America.

We'll either find a way or make one.
Hannibal

The Desire For Change (The Ultimate Power)

What kind of jobs could I get if I could only speak translated, broken English with a strong accent. That inspired me to start looking for opportunities to improve my English fluency.

One day, I watched an advertisement on TV and saw an expert called Fluent English Mr. Wang who guaranteed English fluency. He guaranteed that if you were just starting to learn English and took lessons from him for a year, your English would be more fluent than others who'd learned English for ten years. "How amazing is that?" I thought, but there was a problem. Fluent English Mr. Wang only offered to teach one-on-one private lessons but I didn't have the money. By the way, a private lesson at the time was $30 per hour.

I wondered what Fluent English Mr. Wang did to get that kind of result, but I didn't call him because I thought he wouldn't tell me anyways. Then I thought, "If he can find a way to do it, I can find a way to do it, too!"

So I started by reading books from the library on English fluency. All of the books I intentionally picked were written by native speakers because I thought I should learn from the native. There were lots of words I didn't know but I looked them up in the dictionary.

After I had read about 10 books, I summarized all of the strategies into a list of 10. The strategies were something like "Listen listen listen," "Read read read," "Use what you've learned," "Build your vocabulary," and so on.

I started applying these strategies, and I could understand a little more English but the strategies didn't make me speak any better.

So I kept reading books, and again, all were written by native speakers. But they all said pretty much the same things. I kept reading and reading. As far as I can remember, I read a total of about 60 books, and again all of the books I intentionally picked were written by native speakers, and all of the books said almost the same things.

The strategies were ineffective, so I tried a different approach.

Instead of picking books written by native speakers, all the books I picked this time were written by successful non-native English speakers who had made their English fluent. I picked up and read about 10 of them. To my surprise, all the books said the same things as the 60 books written by native speakers EXCEPT for one thing – Repeat what you hear again and again.

"Repeat what you hear again and again" wasn't mentioned in any of the 60 books written by native speakers at all.

Out of the list of 60 books written by native speakers, one was very useful. This book wasn't about how to speak English fluently. Instead, it was about how to become successful. I came across that book and wondered for three seconds of whether or not to take it. At the last moment, I decided to take it just to take a peek at it in case if there were something useful. To my surprise, it turned out to be a great book on how to set goals and how to become successful. I summarized that book and the ten books written by the successful non-native English speakers and came up with one strategy, a strategy I later named MyFluentEnglish Formula.

The Perfect Opportunity

I was 20 at the time, living in the Brooklyn area of New York City. Every day I took the subway trains to and from Manhattan. The trip took 40 minutes each way on the train. The walk to the train station from home took 12 minutes and the walk from the train station to work took five minutes. All added together, a round trip took an hour and 54 minutes each day. That created a perfect opportunity for me.

I brought my Walkman with me while on the way to work and on the way home. I normally listened to English lessons and sometimes songs, but after I read the last 10 books written by non-native speakers and worked out my strategy, I used the Walkman to try my new strategy – Repeat what you hear again and again.

Taking Action

During these round trips, I first tuned to a news station. It was NPR, National Public Radio, to listen to the news. It worked very well during the 12-minute walk to the train station, but once I entered the train station, the signal was lost. When I got home at night, I recorded the news on a tape for the next day so that I could listen to it on the train. After that, I recorded fresh news every night.

I started by whispering the news, but then I began saying it louder. New York subway trains were as noisy as thunders, and thanks to that! The noise created the perfect opportunity for me to work on my strategy – even the person sitting next to me couldn't hear what I was talking about. So I got to practice the entire train rides both ways.

In the beginning, there were lots of words I didn't understand, but I repeated them anyway! In the beginning, the news was too fast for me, but I repeated what I heard even if I couldn't catch up. Often when there was a word or a phrase I couldn't say, I would rewind the tape and listen to it again. This time, I only listened to it. If I still couldn't say it, I would rewind the tape again and listen again until I could say it. Then I would repeat the word or phrase once, twice, three times … until I could correctly say the new word or phrase. It helped a lot! The next time I heard that same word or phrase, I could correctly say it.

A tape I used to practice English with.

Following Through

Three months later...

I decided to record my own speaking to see how much I had improved because I had heard some people (at least three that I remembered) saying that I spoke good English. So I wrote down some daily conversational phrases and recorded my voice saying them. To my surprise, I DID speak what I wrote down pretty fluently! I could still hear my accent but the accent was much lighter. Compared to other ESL learners, my English was even better!

I got excited about the results and decided to slightly adjust my approach.

The first thing I changed was recording the news once a week, listening and practicing the same English from native speakers for a whole week. At the beginning of the week, there was almost always something I couldn't say. At the end of the week, I'd mastered speaking everything on the whole tape. I was even almost able to recite everything on the tape including words, sentences, tones, flow...

The next week, I recorded a new tape and did the same things for the rest of the week. I did it for a month and mastered four tapes of English taught by native speakers. On week five, I went back to practice the previous four weeks' English with one tape per day. For the remaining days of the week, I practiced the tapes that I had the hardest time with.

Within a month, I'd mastered speaking four tapes of English taught all by native speakers. Each tape was 60 minutes long. Four tapes were 240 minutes of English taught by native speakers.

The Result

Three months later...

As you may have guessed, I recorded my speaking again, and the results were surprising! My accent was gone, my voice was clear, my pronunciation was correct, and my flow was smooth. In other words, my English was fluent!

It was a total of six months that I had spent practicing my English, but the result was overwhelming.

After talking to a friend on the phone for a moment, the friend suddenly asked, " What did you do?" I said, "Huh? What do you mean?" He said, "Your English! It's GOOD!" He said the word "good" with a tone that was so sincere that I could feel the energy of his voice.

Two of my cousins, both native speakers, asked, "How come YOUR English is so good but your brother's and sisters' are not?"

The Continuing Effort

I didn't just stop there. For the months and years that followed, I continued to use my strategy when I found opportunities even though my situation had changed.

Years later I developed yet another strategy I called Open Throat, which I'll talk about in the next chapter. When speaking English with the Open Throat Strategy, my English sounds absolutely 100% native.

When my son was in first grade, he invited me to read to his class as a guest reader. His teacher was so upset because I looked like I couldn't speak English, which would mean disaster for her class. However, his teacher was absolutely stunned when I spoke. I saw her eyes widened for five seconds followed by a long smile. She watched quietly as I inspired her students to enjoy the book by talking with 100% enthusiasm and speaking in 100% native English. She then suddenly jumped into action by whipping out her camera and started taking pictures. She even interrupted me by asking if she could put a picture in her class newsletter. She later asked if I could participate more to help her in her class activities.

3 — How Fluent? One Word: Native!

This is a strategy which I had later developed that brought my fluency to the next level. I called it Open Throat.

When practicing, open your throat, talk with your diaphragm and bring the energy from your stomach.

The energy flow and the way of speaking make a huge difference. To do this, you must open your throat, let the air flow through, and talk with energy from your stomach. You should feel your stomach tighten when you talk.

So bring your energy up all the way from your stomach, let the air flow from your lungs through your throat, and talk with your throat open.

After my daughter joined her school chorus class, she told me that her chorus teacher taught the class the following:

"Open throat!"

Have you ever seen anyone sing with their throat? In other words, singing like that is called singing with a "Chicken Throat." It's far from good. How do you like that?

Are you too nervous to speak English? Are you too shy to speak English? Are you using Chicken Throat to speak English because you're nervous or shy? Because you're afraid you'll make mistakes, so others may laugh at you?

Listen to me: English is a foreign language to you anyway. Making mistakes speaking a foreign language is very normal! Instead, open your throat to speak English. Open your throat and use MyFluentEnglish formula to make you speak English like a native!

Do that for six months, and then, when you speak like me, when you speak English like a native, even native speakers are scared of you, who is going to laugh at you?

It is in the moment of decision that your destiny is shaped.

Anthony Robbins

4 — The Formula To Make You Speak English Like A Native

Here is the formula!

I named the formula MyFluentEnglish Formula. MyFluentEnglish Formula has three steps.

Step 1: Set Your Goal
Step 2: Take Action
Step 3: Follow Through

Step 1: Set Your Goal

Setting your goal is deciding what you want. Congratulations! You've already decided what you want. By getting this book, you're very clear that your Step 1 is to speak English like a native (or at least speak English fluently).

The word "decide" originates from Greek and means to cut off from. Once you've decided on what you want, that's it; you cut off from any other possibility and focus only on what you've decided on.

Decide what you want is like setting a target for you to shoot at.

Clarity is power. The clearer you are on what you want, the more precise your brain takes you to your target. You must know exactly what you want so that you know exactly where to go.

When I used MyFluentEnglish Formula to learn to speak English, I decided that I wanted to speak fluent English. With the target set in place, I started working to reach the target. I worked only on my spare times, but with a target set in sight, I aimed at the target and knew exactly where to go.

If you decide to speak fluent English, go for it. If you decide to speak English like a native, go for it! These are very clear targets.

Once you've decided on exactly what you want, it's critical that you continue focusing on your target. That's "focusing" on your target. The key word is "focusing." You haven't shot any arrows at your target yet. Step 1 is just setting your target in place.

In review, your target is what you want; what you want is your target. With that in mind, you're now ready to take Step 2.

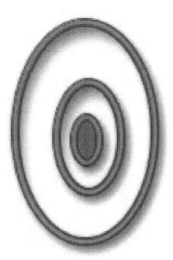

Decide What You Want is like setting a target for you to shoot at.

Step 2: Take Action

Once you have set your target in place, you'll need to take out your bow and arrows and shoot at your target. Once you have decided on what you want, you'll need to get what you want. To get what you want, you'll have to take action.

It does NOT matter what we CAN do; it does matter what we WILL do. After you set your target, in order to get any result, you'll have to shoot at your target.

Look at me in these two situations:

1. If I can speak English like a native speaker, I have a college degree in information technology, I have a graduate degree in space studies, and I live in the United States of America, a free society where everything is possible.

With all of these potential powers, I CAN do a lot of things, but if I DO NOT do anything, nothing will happen.

2. If I speak broken English, I don't have money for private lessons, and I don't have much time to learn English.

With all of these restrictions, I CAN'T do a lot of things to speak fluent English, but if I WILL do something to speak fluent English, I will still achieve some fluency. In fact, with all these restrictions, I did something and made me speak English like a native.

It's not what we are capable of that makes things happen; it's what we WILL do that makes things happen.

When I was 20, I knew I wanted to speak fluent English, and I took action to improve my English. And I DID get excellent results. My action got me exactly what I wanted.

So take action to get what you want. Literally get going to get what you want. I'll show you step-by-step instructions of what action to take.

Shoot at your target. In order to hit your target, you'll need to shoot at your target.

Step 3: Follow Through

Once you've decided on what you want, and you're taking action to do what you want, keep working on it. Follow through until you succeed!

Making you speak English like a native is a job that takes more than a day to do. Keep taking action day-by-day to get there. Start small and keep building your fluency little-by-little, day-by-day.

Let's look at this example. If you want to lift 300 pounds, can you lift 300 pounds? How about 3 pounds? Can you lift 3 pounds? Yes! You can start by lifting 3 pounds day, day-by-day, every day. You keep increasing the amount of weight little-by-little, day-by-day. Before you know it, what seemed impossible before is already possible. You've already built enough muscle to effortlessly lift 300 pounds.

When I started to improve my English, I started by taking one single action. The next day, I took one more action. I kept taking the same action day-by-day. After three months, I had already built enough fluency that people started telling me that my English was good!

I followed through by building my fluency little-by-little, day-by-day. After another three months, I started to speak what seemed impossible before – fluent English!

If you'd build your fluency by just 1% a day and keep building on it, imagine what your fluency will be like six months later . You could have built enough fluency to speak English that seemed impossible before!

Let's review the MyFluentEnglish Formula. The MyFluentEnglish Formula has three steps:

Step 1: Set Your Goal
Step 2: Take Action
Step 3: Follow Through

Life is either a daring adventure or nothing.
Helen Keller

Practicing Kung Fu. Practice was the key to my success.

5 — The One Word Secret

Now that you know the formula, it's time to learn what to do to speak English like a native.

Let's take a look at this:

You want to learn Kung Fu so that you can beat 10 people. You've watched Kung Fu movies and instructional videos. You've also watched how Kung Fu masters beat 10 people. You know the skills you need to know to beat 10 people. Now you're facing 10 people. Can you beat them?

The answer is obvious. If you want to beat 10 people, just knowing how will not let you beat them. In order to beat them, you'll have to practice your Kung Fu. You'll need to build up your muscles, harden your fists, stretch your legs, aim your kicks...

You need to get your mind mentally ready and your bodily mechanisms physically ready to beat 10 people. In order to do that, what you need to do is one word: **practice**.

The same thing applies to speaking English. If you want to speak English like a native, just knowing how to speak will not get you there; you'll have to practice speaking English. I mean literally practice speaking English, over and over again. You need to open your throat, relax your tongue, loosen your muscles, and control your flow...

You need to get your mind mentally ready and your bodily mechanisms physically ready to speak English like a native. In order to do that, what you need to do is one word: **practice**.

There are many places where you can practice. I highly recommend you use all of them whenever possible.

On The Train

If you take the train to work, congratulations! I hope your train is loud so you can follow my exact footsteps – because if your train is too quiet, people will look at you. When I practiced on the train, I found a corner seat to sit down. You can do the same. Find a corner seat and practice your English.

You should speak out loud! You should NOT whisper, because whispering will get you a different result, and that's NOT the result you want. In this digital age, you are lucky! You can take out your cell phone, put on your headphones, and practice just like you would on a phone. The person sitting next to you will think you're talking on the phone.

On The Bus

If you take the bus to work, congratulations! Your bus won't be too loud so it won't damage your hearing. Still, try to speak like you normally would because whispering will get you a different result. Whispering will train your tongue and lips but will not train your throat, your diaphragm, stomach, tone, volume, and airflow. Remember though – in order to be fluent, you'll have to practice in other places where you can speak out loud.

In The Car

This is, by far, my favorite place to practice my English. There is a lot of freedom in the car, and you can go full throttle when practicing.

When I later got the chance to practice in the car, I practiced everything I heard. Since the car was much quieter than the train and no one was sitting next to me, I turned up the volume and followed what I heard with the same tones, same volumes, same flow, same speed, same expressions... exact same everything. In addition, I got to use my hands to help me express my feelings.

I always closed the windows so that people on the street wouldn't be able to hear me. Occasionally I saw people on the street looking at me puzzled. Today, you're lucky. When people on the street look at you, they will just think you're just talking on the phone.

So in short, when practicing in the car, just follow with the same tones, same volumes, same flow, same speed, same expressions, exact same everything at full speed. I do want to stress though; it's speaking you should go full speed on, not driving. So drive safe.

At Home

Do you cook at home? I know I do. I started cooking for the family since I was 7, so I'm very good at it. I even taught my wife how to cook since she'd never cooked before she married me. For me, cooking normally takes 10 minutes for breakfast and 40 minutes for dinner. That's 50 minutes a day. When cooking, your brain is free and it's a perfect time to practice. This is a real good time to put on your headphones and practice.

Outdoors

Outdoor activities such as running, jogging, walking, hiking, and shopping can also be great opportunities for practicing.

At Work

I worked at the Boeing Company for two years where I often worked at the aircraft-building factory. The factory was very noisy, and everyone must wear earplugs in the assembly areas. I used this as an excellent opportunity to practice – I put on my noise-canceling headphones and practiced as loud as I wanted and no one could hear me.

Is your workplace a good place to practice? How many hours do you work a day? If you can put your work hours to good use, you can skyrocket your results.

The successful warrior is the average man with laser-like focus.

Bruce Lee

6 — Get It Right, Baby!

Carefully choosing the correct materials is the key to your success. The materials you choose determine whether you will speak good English, bad English, right English, or wrong English.

I would like you to see this very clearly:

The pronunciations of British English and American English are different. If you want to speak like a native, you want to speak like a native of what? You can't mix the two accents if you want to speak like a native! You must pick only ONE to learn. Either one is fine, but you must pick ONE. Pick one, stick to it, and leave the other one alone. You can go back to other one AFTER you speak one like a native. Before you speak like a native, focus on one.

In other words, if you want to learn to speak British English like a native, pick ALL materials in British English. Likewise, if you want to learn to speak American English like a native, pick ALL materials in American English. Pick one language, British or American, and stick with it!

There are two boats you can catch. Each boat will get you to a different destination, but you can only sit on one boat at a time. So pick a boat and get on it.

You want to speak English like a native, right? Listen to the expert! Pick one. You can understand the other one perfectly well, but to speak like a native, you must pick one and only one.

Remember what Bruce Lee said? Focus!

If unfocused, your laser beam is not strong enough to melt snow, but if focused, your laser beam is strong enough to cut steel!

Take three seconds to think of which accent to learn and then continue reading.

Now that you have chosen your language, it's time to

choose the right materials. Think of it this way:

If you choose materials in which someone is speaking native English, you'll learn to speak native English.

If you choose materials in which someone is speaking incorrect English, you'll learn to speak incorrect English.

If you choose materials in which native speakers are speaking English in real life situations, you'll learn to speak real life English.

If you choose materials in which native speakers are speaking English in unrealistic situations, you'll learn to speak unrealistic English.

...

I remember listening to a tape which a friend was introducing a friend to another friend. The conversation was like this:

"Mr. Wong, this is Mr. Chen, Bill Chen. Mr. Chen, this is Mr. Wong, Dan Wong."

"How do you do?"

"It's my pleasure to meet you."

"Me too!"

This conversation from an old recorded lesson was perfectly correct in English grammar, and the people participating in the conversation were native English speakers. However, this is wrong! Very wrong! Native English speakers don't speak this way. This makes people feel awkward and uncomfortable, and the atmosphere is filled with restrictions. Essentially, the conversation would be unnatural.

In the real world, the conversation would be like this:

"Dan, meet Bill!"

"How's going, Bill?"

"How's going, Dan?"

Notice the "How's going" but not "How's it going?" This is the actual conversation native speakers use when meeting new people. This is a casual, informal conversation that native speakers feel comfortable to take part in.

So if you have lessons from English instructional textbooks or recordings that are not performed by native speakers or are not about real life situations, put them away. Choose something that people actually do use.

Choose these materials:

- All materials performed only by native speakers.
- All English must be naturally spoken in real life situations.
- Pick all materials in ONE accent: British English OR American English.
- Again, learn ONE language and only one language. Either one is fine.

Here are some right materials to use:

- News! Yes, news! Two good examples are BBC News and NPR News. These are real life situations reported to you in direct, clear, and easy to understand English.
- Learning sites: For British English, BBC Learning is an excellent choice. Here is a shortened URL http://tinyurl.com/qqq3333. For American English, Voice of America Learning is an excellent one. Here is a shortened URL http://tinyurl.com/qqq3334.
- Audio story books! This is, by far, my favorite source. Listen to stories with lots of action. There, you can pickup English vocabulary words quickly. Pick ALL audio story books written by native writers and read by native speakers.
- Movies. With pictures, movies are easy to understand.
- Your choice of your favorite materials performed by

native speakers in real life situations.

Concerning all acts of initiative and creation there is one elementary truth — that the moment one definitely commits oneself then divine providence moves too.

William Hutchinson Murray

7 — This Is Your Right Hand Man

When I practiced my English, I didn't spend a dime. I used the Walkman and the pair of cheap headphones that I already had.

Today, you're lucky. You can use your cell phone and a pair of cheap headphones. If you drive, link up your cell phone with your car via Bluetooth and use the speakers of the car. If you don't have a cell phone, that's fine. You can use an MP3 player or other playing devices.

When I practiced my English on subway trains, the subway trains were so loud that I turned up the volume in order to hear what was playing. I remember so clearly that I turned the volume up to 10 and the highest volume on that Walkman was 10. In noisy areas, a pair of noise-canceling headphones is a good choice since turning the volume up too high can damage your hearing.

There are two new headphones available today. One is over-the-ear noise-canceling headphones, and the other is in-ear isolation headphones. These headphones are good only for noisy areas. It's best to use regular headphones or no headphones.

Over-the-ear Noise-canceling headphones filter out what you don't want to hear and let you hear what you do want to hear at low volume. The headphones detect outside noise and generate sound waves in the opposite frequency, flattening the outside noise, making it inaudible to you.

I own a pair of Audio-Technica headphones I bought on Amazon. These headphones can block off about 70% of background noise, making my audio clear enough to keep the volume low even in noisy areas. I've also checked out a pair of high-end Bose headphones that were described as much better in performance. According to the report, the headphones can block off about 90% of background noise.

However, these headphones cost three times as much as the Audio-Technica headphones. I've also tried a pair of low-end headphones that a coworker had at Boeing. The price was $30 cheaper than my Audio-Technica headphones, but the quality was bad. It only blocked off about 40-50% of background noise.

In-ear isolation headphones are small, light, and easy to take with you. They're good for outdoor activities. These headphones are, by far, cheaper than over-the-ear noise-canceling headphones.

Make sure you hear me: use these noise-canceling headphones or noise-isolation headphones ONLY if you absolutely need them. You can practice much better without headphones or with a pair of regular headphones. You can speak much better if you can hear what you say.

Nature has placed mankind under the governance of two sovereign masters, pain and pleasure. It is for them alone to point out what we ought to do, as well as to determine what we shall do.
Jeremy Bentham

8 — Step-By-Step Instructions – Let's Make You Speak Like A Native!

Let's review! MyFluentEnglish Formula has three steps.

Step 1: Set Your Goal
Step 2: Take Action
Step 3: Follow Through

Let's do Step 1: Set your goal!

If there is only one thing that you want to take from this book, this is it.

Yes. This is the single most important thing in this entire book.

Let's continue.

Step one is set your goal.

Set a solid goal, a stone goal, an iron goal, a strong goal..., a goal that WILL get you going, a goal that WILL push you forward, a goal that WILL burn your desire to make you speak English like a native.

There are two effective ways to set your goal: inspiration and desperation.

For me it was easy. "What kind of jobs could I get if I could only speak translated, broken English with a strong accent?" That was it! I didn't want to work in a restaurant doing labor work for life. My uncle already found me a job working as an assistant chef at the restaurant he worked. For me, it was desperation: If I don't do anything about my broken English, I'd be doing labor work for life. BUT if I improve my English and speak English fluently, I'd be doing office work and live a much more comfortable life.

That was a small reason, but it was a strong enough reason to push me forward. What is yours?

Here are some examples of inspiration:

"I have a much better background than Ken. If he can make him speak English like a native, I can make me speak English like a native. I WILL make me speak English like a native. Let me take action now!"

"If Ken, a country boy, a middle school dropout, started at age 20, for six months, can speak English like a native, I can definitely speak English like a native! I WILL make me speak English like a native in six months period!"

Here are some examples of desperation:

66

"If I keep speaking English like this, I'm going to be doing labor work for life. BUT if I speak English like a native, I'm going to live a comfortable life."

"If I don't speak English like a native, I'm never going to get that dream job. BUT if I speak English like a native, not only will I get that dream job, I'll have enough money to move out of this apartment and buy that house on top of the hill."

For desperation, you need to have two parts to make it work. Part one: the pain you have if you don't speak English well. AND part two: the pleasure you'll get if you speak English well. When you have these two parts, your goal works extremely well.

Use whatever you can think of that will inspire you...

Use whatever you can think of that you desperately need...

......

Write down your goal! Yes, write it down. Write down your goal and put it somewhere you can see it VERY OFTEN!

Write down your goal and look at it as often as you can.

I wrote down my goals and placed them on the ceiling in my bedroom right above my bed. I also put a copy on the wall beside my bed. I also put a copy on my desk. I also put a copy in my wallet.

Put your goal in places where you can see them as often as possible. The point here is for you to look at your goal as often as possible to remind you that you have a goal to work on!

80/20

This is the golden rule for success: 80% of your success depends on your goal and 20% on your work.

Once again, if there is only one thing that you want to

take from this book, this is it. This is the single most important thing for your success. If you have your 80%, there are lots of different ways for you to get there. Without your 80%, what are you going to do your other 20% for?

......

A man got fired from his company. He got SO mad that he opened a company to compete with the company that fired him.

The man set a goal, then he worked toward the goal, and in just a few short years he beat the company that fired him. His company today is worth $112 billion.

The man's name is Thomas Watson. The company is IBM.

......

A man got fired from his company. He set a goal to open his own business. He sent an application and a business plan to a bank for a £100,000 loan. The bank asked him to send 16 copies of his plan. He got excited and sent 16 copies of his plan. He never heard from the bank again, so he called the bank. This is the answer he got from the bank:

"We never wanted to lend you the money. We asked for 16 copies your plan to show our employees what a dumb plan is."

The man tried eight other banks, and all refused to lend him money. With a goal set in mind, he tried the ninth bank, and he got the loan. The bank told him that his plan was a very bad plan, but the loan was approved because the loan officer was going to retire in two weeks so whether or not he could pay back the loan didn't to matter him.

The man then set up his business, and with a goal in mind, he was incredibly successful. He paid back the loan in full and sold his business for £47 million. The company that bought his business was WH Smith, the company that

68

fired him.

The man's name is Tim Waterstone. The business he opened is the British bookstore empire, Waterstones.

......

Let me say this again.

If there is only one thing that you want to take from this book, this is it.

Yes. This is the single most important thing in this entire book.

If you haven't read my background yet, read it now. Because with a humble background like that and I can still set a goal and successfully made me speak English like a native, tell yourself this: Yes, I can!

There was one simple reason for me to set a goal that pushed me forward to learn to speak like a native. The more reasons you can find, the better. If all you can find is just one reason, that is enough. Find a reason why you must speak English like a native. Not you want, not you need, not you should, but you MUST. A reason so strong that you must do it. Find that reason now. Then set your goal.

Deep within man dwell those slumbering powers; powers that would astonish him, that he never dreamed of possessing; forces that would revolutionize his life if aroused and put into action.
Orison Swett Marden

Let's do Step 2: Take Action!

To speak English like a native, you'll need to learn from the native, but how to learn from the native is the key. In this step, I'm going to show you how.

Remember the Kung Fu example I mentioned earlier? If you want to be good at Kung Fu, you're going to have to practice Kung Fu. If you want to be good at English, you're going to have to practice English.

So how are you going to learn from the native? Practice.

I'm going to show you nine action to completely get rid of your accent and make you speak English just like a native. So have your MP3 player or your cell phone ready. Put on your headphones if you need. Go to one of the following links to download a native study material.

For American English, download this one: http://tinyurl.com/qqq4444.

For British English, download this one: http://tinyurl.com/qqq4445.

Just type either one of the above links on your web browser, and the native study material will be automatically downloaded to your computer. Remember, download only one and leave the other one alone.

Now let's take Action 1.

Action 1: Listen And Repeat At The Same Time

Listen to this audio and repeat what you hear immediately. I mean immediately. Right at the moment you hear it.

I would like to stress the importance of this. When you hear the beginning of a sentence, you repeat the beginning of the sentence. When you hear the middle of a sentence, you repeat the middle of the sentence. When you hear the end of a sentence, you repeat the end of the sentence. Whenever you hear something, repeat that immediately.

In other words, repeat what you hear as quickly as you can. What you're doing here is naturally building your fluency. You're doing this to train your brain, your mouth, your tongue, your lips, your throat, your lungs, your stomach ... and everything you need to speak English NATURALLY without first translating it! So just say what you hear immediately. Let the meaning, the grammar, the vocabulary ... and everything else build subconsciously.

At the beginning of your practice, if you hear words you don't know how to say or words that are hard to say, that's perfectly fine. Just try to say the words or just make some noise and move on.

Action 2: Finish Repeating The Whole Material

Listen to and repeat the whole material from the beginning straight to the end. If you have to pause it, pause it. When you come back, keep going from where you've left off. What you're doing here is building your flow, making you speak whole sentences instead of just words, so repeat whole sentences and the whole material from the beginning to the end.

Again, if you come across something you can't say correctly or can't say at all, that's fine – just make some noise and move on. Remember, even if there are words you can't say, keep on going forward. Continue all the way to the end.

Action 3: Record Your Voice

Yes, record your voice practicing this piece of native study material. This is crucial. Do NOT skip this.

Now you know how to practice the repeating strategy, and you have already repeated this material once. At this point, you'll need to record your own voice repeating this same piece of material. So find a recording device such as your computer, another cell phone, or other recording device and record your voice.

By the way, you'll need to put on a pair of headphones to listen to the native study material this time so that you can record your voice clearly. So listen to the native study material through your headphones this time. Find a recording device such as your computer, another cell phone, or other recording device and record your voice doing the following:

Record your voice repeating the whole material from the beginning to the end.

Repeat everything you know how to say and make some noise on everything you don't know how to say. Just do your best and keep on going forward.

Remember to keep going straight forward until you get to the end. Save your voice file and leave it alone. You will listen to it later.

Action 4: Finish Repeating The Whole Material All At Once Yet Another Time

For the third time, listen to and repeat the same material from the beginning right to the end. You want to keep your flow going – repeat the full sentences and the whole material. Repeat everything you know how to say and make some noise on everything you don't know how to say. Just do your best and keep going forward until you reach the end.

Action 5: Go Back And Repeat The Words You Can't Say For As Many Times As You Need

Now that you have listened to and repeated this single file three times and you know the sentence flow. It's time to listen to and repeat the same thing again. This time, immediately go back to the words you can't say. Listen to them again and try to say them again. Try to say them again and listen to them again. Try once, twice, three times.... Try as many times as you need UNTIL you can say them correctly.

Action 6: Finish Repeating The Whole Material N Times

Now that you know how to say every word in this piece of native study material. It's time to practice the whole thing again. From the beginning to the end, practice saying what you hear for as many times as needed. Be sure to practice the flow, the tones, the volumes, the expressions, the speed... Practice everything you hear.

Practice this piece of native study material for as many times and you need until you can say it naturally.

Action 7: Record Your English

Congratulations for getting this far! Now it's time to record your voice again repeating the same piece of native study material. Take out your recording device and record yourself repeating the very same piece of material you've been practicing. Save your voice file.

Now it's time to compare your recordings. Listen to the first recording first and then listen to the second recording. How do you like your English in the beginning? How do you like your English now? Do you hear any improvement?

If you don't hear any improvement, that's fine. This piece of native study material may not be a good fit for you, or you may be too good for this piece of native study material. Let's move on. Take Action 8.

If you do hear an improvement, congratulations, you ARE speaking better than before. Let's do even better than that! Move on.

Is your English as good as the speaker? If your English is as good as the speaker, good job! You are beginning to speak like a native! Keep up the good work! Let's take Action 8.

Action 8: Find A Different Piece Of Material And Do Action 1 To 7

First, let's rate this native study material. Choose one of the following. To me, this native study material is:

1. Too slow.
2. Just right.
3. Too fast.

Choice 3: Too fast. If you chose 3, congratulations! That's very normal! Go to one of the following links, pick a different native study material at a slower speed, use the new native study material and do action 1 to 7 again.

Slower speed for American English: http://tinyurl.com/qqq4446

Slower speed for British English: http://tinyurl.com/qqq5551

Choice 2: Just right. If you chose 2, congratulations! You're almost there! You'll be speaking like a native very soon. Go to one of the following, pick a different native study material at the same speed, use the new native study material and do action 1 to 7 again.

Average speed for American English: http://tinyurl.com/qqq4447

Average speed for British English: http://tinyurl.com/qqq5552

Choice 1: Too slow. If you chose 1, congratulations! Your English speed is too good. Unless you really want to speak faster than an average native English speaker, go back to Choice 2, pick a different native study material, use the new native study material and do action 1 to 7 again. If you still want to speak faster than an average native English speaker, go to one of the following links, pick a different native study material at ultra fast speed, use the new native study material and do action 1 to 7 again.

Ultra fast speed for American English:

81

http://tinyurl.com/qqq4448
Ultra fast speed for British English:
http://tinyurl.com/qqq5553

Give me a lever long enough and a fulcrum on which to place it, and I can single-handedly move the Earth.

Archimedes

Let's do Step 3: Follow Through!

Keep doing Step 2! This is Step 3! Keep taking action 1 to 8. This is how you follow through to get the results you've been waiting for.

Once a month, go back to the previous pieces of native study materials you've practiced before and try to practice them again. This is for your retention. Go back to them and practice them again. This will help your brain naturally memorize them and your bodily mechanisms naturally speak them!

Here is something to get excited about: By taking action 1 to 8, your brain will NATURALLY process the pronunciation, grammar, sentence flow, speed, tone, vocabulary ... and everything you need to speak like a native on whatever you practice. As a result, you'll know exactly how to correctly pronounce English words, you'll know exactly when to start, when to pause and when to stop, you'll know exactly what to say louder and what to say softer, you'll know exactly when to speak faster and when to speak slower ... just like native speakers would.

This step will bring you the results you've been waiting for! If there is one word to describe this step, the word is "persistence." Keep building on top of what you've been building to achieve what you want.

By the way, here is a reminder: Open Throat!

That's it! Follow through and you WILL get there!

Reason guides but a small part of man, and the rest obeys feeling, true or false, and passion, good or bad.

Joseph Roux

9 — Your Road To Success

Fun fact:

One percent (Yes, 1%) of people who buy instructional books follow the instructions in the books and succeed. The other 99% will put the books away and search for other books or do nothing else and never succeed on what they wanted. That's the reason why for every 100 people who want to learn to speak English like a native, one person will succeed.

Are you going to be the 99% who will put this book away and buy other books or the 1% who'll stop searching, follow the instructions in this book, keep working on it, and finally speak English like a native?

How much you'll succeed is up to you. Following the step-by-step instructions in this book will get you off a good start, AND persistence will give you success. Give yourself a chance to succeed by taking action and giving yourself time to succeed. Now, follow my proven MyFluentEnglish Formula and take action to produce your results!

What you need to do is to take action today. The key word is today. Copy my formula today and follow the exact same process I've done before. Start from today – I mean today, right now. Do exactly what I've before. Take one action to start building your fluency today.

You only need to start from small and keep building.

Can you lift 100 kg? It's too heavy for most of us. Can you lift 2 kg? Yes, you can. Let's start by lifting 2 kg today, 3 kg tomorrow, and keep adding. By doing this, your muscles will continue to build, and before you know it, you've already built enough muscles to effortless lift weight that seemed impossible before!

Started at age 20 for six months, if I, a country boy, a middle school dropout with no special talent, can learn to

89

speak English like a native, my friend, yes, you can!
Take action now and keep building!

Lesson 1 (with Free Audio & Video)

English Pronunciation
Pronounce English Words Like A Pro In 6 Months

Volume 1

Ken Xiao

Download your free audio and video at

http://www.myfluentenglish.com/esl/verifypurchase

Chapter 1: Two Free Bonuses

By getting this book, you get two **big** bonuses for free.

These big bonuses are your tickets to success. Use them and use them well.

Bonus 1: Free Video.
Bonus 2: Free Audio.

The free video starts from chapter four. It's designed to teach you on how to pronounce the focused words in this lesson correctly.

Download the video files and do two things:

1. Watch and listen to how native speakers pronounce the words.
2. Repeat what you see and hear again and again.

Watch and listen to them not once, not twice, not three times, but as many times as you need.
Repeat what you hear not once, not twice, not three times, but again and again as many times as you need until you can pronounce every word in this lesson correctly.

The free audio also starts from chapter four. The first parts of the audios are recorded at a slower speed for you to get the pronunciation right. The second parts of the audios are recorded at a normal conversational speed for you to learn to speak naturally. If others have been telling you to speak slowly and clearly, they have meant with the best intentions. However, exactly the opposite is what you need. You need to listen to English at a normal conversational speed, and you need to speak English at a normal conversational speed. You can achieve that by following my step-by-step instructions in the next chapter.

Download the audio files and do two things:

1. Listen to them chapter by chapter
2. Repeat what you hear again and again

Listen to them not once, not twice, not three times, but as many times as you need.

Repeat what you hear not once, not twice, not three times, but again and again as many times as you need until you can speak every word and every sentence correctly, fluently, and naturally.

Here is the link to your free audio and video again:

http://www.myfluentenglish.com/esl/verifypurchase

I fear not the man who has practiced 10,000 kicks once, but I fear the man who has practiced one kick 10,000 times.
Bruce Lee

Chapter 2: Step-By-Step Instructions

Focus! These instructions are rewritten specifically for this lesson.

If it's unfocused, your laser beam can't even melt snow, but if it's focused, the same laser beam can cut steel!

Learn from the success. Focus on this lesson to first make you speak this lesson like a native and then expand to other lessons. Follow my proven step-by-step instructions to get your results.

Listen to the audio of chapter 4 and do the following.

Step 1: Listen And Repeat At The Same Time

Listen to this audio and repeat what you hear immediately. Do not wait until the end. Repeat immediately.

Step 2: Finish Repeating The Whole Audio

Listen to and repeat this audio from the beginning to the end.

Step 3: Record Your Voice

Record your voice repeating this audio. This is important. Do NOT skip it.

Find a recorder such as your computer, another cell phone or an MP3 recorder. Put on a pair of headphones and record your voice repeating this audio from the beginning to the end.

Save the file and move on to Step 4.

Step 4: Finish Repeating This Audio One More Time

Listen to and repeat this chapter again from the

beginning to the end.

Step 5: Go Back And Repeat The Words You Can't Say For As Many Times As You Need

Repeat this chapter again. This time stop and go back to the words you can't say. Listen again and repeat. Try once, twice, three times... Repeat as many times as you need until you can say the words correctly.

Step 6: Finish Repeating This audio For As Many Times As You Need

Now repeat this chapter from the beginning to the end. Repeat once, twice, three times... Repeat as many times as you need until you can say each sentence naturally and fluently.

Step 7: Record Your Voice

Now record your voice again. Record your voice repeating this chapter. Save your voice file.

Find the first recording and listen to it.
Find the second recording and listen to it.

Did you speak better in the second recording than in the first recording?

Yes? Let's take Step 8.
No? Let's take Step 8.

Step 8: Move On To The Next Chapter

Listen to the audio of the next chapter and take steps 1 – 7.

After you finish the entire book, go back to

chapter 4 and start over again until you're satisfied with your result.

Stay focused.
Brandon T. Adams

Chapter 3: Learn The Most Useful Words

The English vocabulary has over 500,000 words, but .1% (Yes. 0.1%) of these words make up 80% of daily conversation. In this lesson, we're going to learn the most useful words. Following are the top 100 most useful words in the English language.

Rank	Word	Rank	Word
1	the	26	from
2	of	27	or
3	to	28	had
4	and	29	by
5	a	30	hot
6	in	31	but
7	is	32	some
8	it	33	what
9	you	34	there
10	that	35	we
11	he	36	can
12	was	37	out
13	for	38	other
14	on	39	were
15	are	40	all
16	with	41	your
17	as	42	when
18	I	43	up
19	his	44	use
20	they	45	word
21	be	46	how
22	at	47	said
23	one	48	an
24	have	49	each
25	this	50	she

Rank	Word	Rank	Word
51	which	76	more
52	do	77	day
53	their	78	could
54	time	79	go
55	if	80	come
56	will	81	did
57	way	82	my
58	about	83	sound
59	many	84	no
60	then	85	most
61	them	86	number
62	would	87	who
63	write	88	over
64	like	89	know
65	so	90	water
66	these	91	than
67	her	92	call
68	long	93	first
69	make	94	people
70	thing	95	may
71	see	96	down
72	him	97	side
73	two	98	been
74	has	99	now
75	look	100	find

Let's learn these words one by one and then in context to speak these most useful words correctly, fluently, and naturally like a native speaker.

FOCUS
Follow One Course Until Successful
Anonymous

Chapter 4: 1 – 10, My First Day Of School In New York

#1: the
Pronounced T̲Hə

Put your tongue between your upper and lower front teeth and then release your tongue to pronounce the word.

- the world
- the book
- the house
- the tree
- the computer
- the yummy food

- There are 7.2 billion people in the world.
- The tree is in front of the house.
- The book is next to the computer.
- The teacher is very happy to teach me.

When the is in front of a vowel (a, e, i, o, u), then the is pronounced as thee.
- the apple
- the elephant
- the ice
- the other
- the umbrella

- The apple tree is in the front of the house.
- The elephant is playing with the umbrella.

- The ice in this lake is melting, but the ice in the other lake is still frozen.
- The English teacher of this lesson is a successful person because he focuses on what he wants.

- Do you have the key?
- I don't have "the" key. I have "a" key.

#2: of
Pronounced əv
The letter "f" in this word is pronounced as "v."

- 1 of 2.
- North of New York.
- The United States Of America.
- 100 of 500,000 English words.
- Chapter four of this book.

- The English language is one of the biggest languages in the world.
- One of my friends is an English teacher.
- Toronto is in the north of New York.
- English is the official language of the United States.
- The audio of this book starts from chapter four.
- If I follow the instructions of the book, I will pronounce every one of these words correctly.

#3, to

Pronounced too

- To learn English.
- Come to my house.
- Go to school.
- To the west.
- To be closed.
- To people.

- I'd love to learn to speak English well.
- To successfully learn to speak English, you must speak English.
- I asked her to come to my house, but she said she didn't want to.
- Seattle is 3000 miles to the west of New York.
- It's five to ten (Its five minutes to 10 O'clock).
- My car does 40 miles to the gallon.
- He pulled the door to behind him.
- I'm nice to everybody.

#4, and
Pronounced and

- A pen and a paper.
- Milk and cheese.
- Love and marriage.
- Rabbit and carrots.
- Come and go.
- The first and the second.

- Do you have a pen and a paper?
- Milk and cheese make you grow tall.
- They say love and marriage are like horse and carriage. I say love and marriage are like rabbit and carrots.
- He turned around and left.
- The first one is a boy, and the second one is a girl.
- My English is getting better and better.
- Three and seven make ten (3 + 7 = 10)

#5, a
Pronounced ə

- A train.
- A girl.
- A computer.
- A book.
- A seat.

- A train is coming.
- A girl walks on the train.
- She sits on a seat at the corner and takes out a book.
- She then takes out a computer.

#6, in
Pronounced in

- In the house.
- In the year 2016.
- Come in.
- locked in.
- I'm in.
- See you in 15 minutes.
- She's in love with him.
- It's in the book.
- Say it in English.

- In the year 2016, my one-year old niece locked herself in the house by accident, and no one had the key to go in.
- Do you want to play basketball in the afternoon? Sure! I'm in! See you in 15 minutes.
- She's in love with you. If you love her, go to her and say "I love you" in English.
- It works like chemical. I learned it in the book.

#7, is
Pronounced iz

- This is wonderful.
- He is in school.
- Barack Obama is from Chicago.
- This apple is 25 cents.
- One and one is two. (1 + 1 = 2)
- She's everything to him.

- Chicago is 12 hours west of New York.
- Barack Obama is from Chicago.
- He's in school. His school is PS 101.
- One and one is two. Two and two is four.
- Apples are on sale today. This apple is 25 cents.
- He loves her so much that she's everything to him.

#8, it
Pronounced it

- In it.
- It's me.
- What time is it?
- It's OK.
- It's easy.
- We are it.

- The glass has water in it.
- Who is it? It's me.
- What time is it? It's 3:30.
- "I'm sorry." "It's OK."
- "Did you finish the homework today?" "Yes. It's easy."
- "Where is the rescue team?" "We're it."

#9, you
Pronounced yo̅o̅

- How are you?
- You students.
- You confident people.
- You get used to it.

- How are you? Fine. Thanks.
- Are you OK? Yes. I'm OK.
- Do you take the subway train to work? Yes. I do.
- You students will take the SAT before entering college.
- You confident people will get by easily.
- Gas price has doubled in the past few years, but after a while, you get used to it.

#10, that
Pronounced THat

- Who's that?
- That's a good idea?
- The word that you've just learned.
- The year that I came to America.
- I took the subway train at that time.
- Where's that boy of yours.
- Go that far.
- More than that.
- She said that .

- Who's that? That's a new student.
- Let's talk to him in English." "That's a good idea.
- The word that you've just learned is you.
- The day that I came to America it was snowing.
- I took the subway train to school at that time.
- Where's that boy of yours?
- Not only would I go that far, I would even do more than that.
- She said that she wanted to learn English.

Now let's use these 10 words!

- My name is Hassan.
- I'm from Saudi Arabia.
- The day that I came to America it was snowing.
- The apple tree in front of the house was covered by snow.
- There were two lakes near the house.
- The ice in the small lake was melting, but the ice in the other lake was still frozen.

- I took the subway train to school at that time.
- When I was waiting on the platform, I saw a beautiful girl wearing a pair of headphones.
- When a train came, the girl walked on the train.
- She sat on a seat at a corner and took out a book.
- She tapped on the screen of her cellphone and started to read.

- "Who's that?" When I entered the classroom, I heard someone said.
- "That's a new student." Someone else said.
- "Let's talk to him."
- "That's a good idea."
- So two people came to talk to me in English.
- I only knew a little bit of English, so it was hard for me to understand.
- "Do you have a pen and a paper?" One of them asked.
- "Pen? Paper?" I said.
- "Yes. Pen and paper."
- "Yes." I said and took out a pen and a notebook.
- They started talking to me and drawing pictures on

the notebook for what I didn't understand.

- Class soon started.
- Mr. Xiao, the English teacher, taught me something that was shocking to me.
- He said, "The English language is one of the biggest languages in the world. English is the official language of 54 countries. English is the official language of the United States."
- He then said, "The English language has 500,000 words, but .1% make up 80% of daily conversation."
- He then said, "To successfully learn to speak English, you must speak English."

- I'd love to learn to speak English well, so I wanted to talk to the two classmates in English.
- Suddenly, I saw the beautiful girl whom I saw on the train.
- She was in the same class and I didn't notice that!
- I asked her to come to my house, but she said she didn't want to.

- Soon my English was getting better and better, and I felt more comfortable to talk in English.
- I felt so in love with the girl that I wanted to talk to her.
- "What's the word that we've just learned?" I asked.
- "The word that we've just learned is you," she said.
- "What time is it?" I asked.
- "It's five to three," she said.
- "Do you want to come to my house?" I asked.
- "No," she said.
- The two classmates asked me to play basketball in

the afternoon.

Focus on where you want to go, not what you fear.
Anthony Robbins

Chapter 5: 11 – 20, My First Year In America

#11, he

Pronounced hē

A boy, a man → he
A girl, a woman → she

- Who is he?
- He's a good boy.

- He's an ESL student.
- He's a good kid.
- Hello, may I speak to Hassan, please? This is he.
- Everyone likes my father. He's a happy person.
- The boy knows he's loved.

#12, was

Pronounced wɑz
Today → is
Yesterday → was

- There was a way in.
- There was a boy running to school.
- The test was yesterday.
- The classroom was on his left.
- It was raining until 10.

- Our English test was yesterday.
- It was raining, but there was a boy running to school.
- He walked passed the classroom. It was on his left.
- The classroom was locked, but there was a way in.

#13, for

Pronounced for

- This is for you.
- Are you voting for Hilary or Trump?
- She's leaving for Houston.
- A for apple B for boy.
- Three for a dollar.
- She's tall for her age.
- He was in school for eight hours.
- I run for three miles a day.
- She got 100 on the test for the third time.

- Twenty sixteen is the year to vote for the next president.
- Are you voting for Hilary or Trump?
- Hilary is leaving for Houston.
- H for Hilary T for Trump.
- Apples are three for a dollar.
- Oranges are a dollar for four.
- She stayed in school for eight hours yesterday and got 100 on the test for the third time.

#14, on

Pronounced ôn

- On the stage.
- A smile on your face.
- The lid on the bottle.
- Write it down on paper.
- On the way.
- The test is on Wednesday.
- Lunch is on me.

- Hilary Clinton and Donald Trump are on the stage.
- They both have a smile on their face.
- Hilary drinks some water and puts the lid on the bottle.
- Trump writes down something on paper.
- They're on their way to presidency.

#15, are

Pronounced är

1 → is
2 or more → are
you → are
they → are

- There is a bus.
- There are two buses.
- She is running for president.
- They are running for president.
- How are you?
- This car is red. These cars are white.

- Hilary is running for president.
- Hilary and Trump are running for president.
- There is one bus in Hilary's team.
- There are two buses in Trump's team.

#16, with

Pronounced wiTH

- The girl with a flag.
- A book with a bookmark.
- Fill it with water.
- Fight with each other.
- Do it with pleasure.
- Angry with each other.
- Her student is with her.

- The little girl with a flag is waving.
- She fills the bottle with water.
- Hilary Clinton and Donald Trump are fighting with each other for presidency.
- Are you with Hilary or with Trump?

#17, as

Pronounced az

- As many as 22 people ran for president.
- Trump watches as Hilary speaks.
- Talk as you would if you were the winner.
- I want to start now as I want to get it done as soon as possible.
- He worked as a chef.
- He works as a director.

- As many as 22 candidates ran for president in 2016.
- Hilary is talking as she were the winner.
- Trump is watching as Hilary is speaking.
- America is the land of opportunities. Any thing as wild as you can imagine is possible.
- Two years ago, he worked as a chef, but now he works as the director of business operations.
- Twenty years ago, Ken lived his life as a country boy, a middle school dropout, and a humble man. Now, he lives his life as a winner!

#18, I

Pronounced i

- I'm Angela.
- I'm from Germany.
- I run for three miles a day.
- I'm a student.

#19, his

Pronounced hiz

- Victor came to America with his parents.
- This is his apartment.
- This is his book.
- His English is improving day-by-day.

#20, they

Pronounced THā
One person → he/she
Two or more people → they
One object → it
Two or more objects → they

- They looked confident.
- They are running for president.
- They set their goal years before.
- Ask someone if they wanted to vote.

- Two new students came today. They looked confident.
- Hilary and Trump are successful leaders. They are running for president.
- They set their goal years before to become president. They lay out their plan and take actions.
- Their supporters ask people if they wanted to vote for them.

Now let's use these 10 words.

- I'm Angela.
- I'm a student.
- I came from Germany.
- I came to America with my parents.
- Everyone likes my father. He's a happy person.
- I'm surprised to learn that food is very cheap in America.
- Apples are three for a dollar.
- Oranges are a dollar for four.

- I walk for a mile to school.
- Our English test was yesterday.
- It was raining until 10, but there was a boy running to school.
- He walked passed the classroom. It was on his left.
- The classroom was locked, but there was a way in.
- He stayed in school for eight hours yesterday and got 100 on the test for the third time.

- Twenty sixteen is the year to elect the next president of the United States.
- As many as 22 candidates ran for president.
- Hilary was talking as she were the winner.
- Trump was watching as Hilary spoke.
- Hilary and Trump are successful leaders.
- They set their goal years before to become president. They lay out their plan and take actions to achieve their goal.

- Hilary was leaving for Houston.
- There was one bus in Hilary's team.

- There were two buses in Trump's team.
- There was a little girl with a flag waving at them.
- Hilary Clinton and Donald Trump were on the stage.
- They both had a smile on their face.
- Hilary drank some water and put the lid on the bottle.
- Trump wrote down something on paper.
- They were on their way to presidency.
- There are posters everywhere.
- H for Hilary and T for Trump.
- Are you voting for Hilary or Trump?

The successful warrior is the average man with laser-like focus.
Bruce Lee

Chapter 6: 21 – 30, My First Job in Arizona

#21, be

Pronounced bē

- Six apples will be $2.
- I'll be there.
- It'll be this way.
- Will you be my friend?
- I'll be there.

#22, at

Pronounced at

- Arrive at 250 Main Street.
- Starts at eight o'clock.
- It's cooler at night.
- At home, at work, at school.
- At age 7.
- Good at math.
- Look at that.

- I arrived at 250 Main Street at five o'clock.
- It was cooler at night, so I brought a jacket.
- I started to work at seven.
- I'm always learning at home, at work, and at school.
- I'm good at math.

#23, one

Pronounced wən

- One person.
- One of my goals.
- One day in October.

- One of my goals is to speak English fluently.
- I practice with one of my friends.
- One day I'm going to speak English fluently.

#24, have

Pronounced həv

Today → have
Yesterday → had
For some time → have been

- I have a new friend.
- How many brothers and sisters do you have?
- They have two stores.
- He had two drinks.
- They had fun.
- They have been friends for 20 years.
- I have been to America for two years.

#25, this

Pronounced THis

One → this
Two or more → these

- This book.
- These books.
- This month.
- This year.
- This is.

- This is your book.
- These are their books.
- This book is yours.
- These books are theirs.
- This will be an easy week.
- Hello, may I speak to Jack, please?
- Who's this? This is Victor.

#26, from

Pronounced frəm

- From here.
- From 9 - 5.
- From now on.
- From Monday to Friday.
- From no English to fluent English.

- Work hours are from nine to five.
- Work days are from Monday to Friday.
- From now on, I work eight hours a day.
- I came from Korea.

#27, or

Pronounced ôr

- This or that.
- Tea or water?
- One or two.
- Use it or loose it.
- Is this yours or his?

- Would you like this one or that one?
- Tea or water? Water, please.
- Would you like one pound or two pounds? Two pounds, please.
- We either use our skills or loose our skills.

#28, had

Pronounced həd
Today → have
Yesterday → had
For some time → have been

- I had water.
- She had tea.
- They had a few drinks.
- They had fun in Arizona.

- What did you have? I had water.
- What did she have? She had tea.
- How many books do you have? I have two.
- How much water did you have yesterday? I had eight bottles.

#29, by

Pronounced bī

- A book by Ken Xiao.
- What do you go by?
- By bus. By train. By subway.
- Homework is due by Monday.
- Pass by your house.

- This book is written by Ken Xiao.
- What do you go by? I go by Jack.
- How do you go to work? By bus.
- This project is due by Monday.
- I drove by your house this morning.
- I'll stop by today.

#30, hot

Pronounced hät

- Arizona is hot in the summer.
- A hot dish.
- Hot pepper.
- This is an hot issue.

- In Arizona, summer temperature ranges from 90 to 110 degrees. It's really hot for me.
- This dish is cooked with chili pepper. Is it hot for you?
- The Super Bowl is a hot game in America.

It's that time again. Let's learn these words in context.

- My name is Yoon-Jin.
- My parents and relatives called me Yoon-Jin.
- I go by Jack in school and at work.
- I came from Korea.
- In Arizona, summer is really cold at night and really hot during the day. Temperature ranges from 50 to 110 degrees.
- In my first day of work, I arrived at 250 Main Street at eight o'clock.
- Work hours were from eight thirty to five.
- Work days were from Monday to Friday.
- It has been this way, but from now on, work hours are from nine to five.
- It's cooler in the morning and at night, so I always bring a jacket.
- I work at a grocery store.
- Once a customer asked me how much were the apples she had on her hand.
- Since apples were a dollar for three, and she had six apples on her hand, I said, "Six apples will be $2."
- I'm good at math.
- That was easy for me.
- One of my goals is to speak English fluently.
- I practice with one of my friends.
- One day I'm going to speak English fluently.

We'll either find a way or make one.
Hannibal

Chapter 7: 31 – 40, The World

#31, but

Pronounced bət

- Some countries are small, but some countries are big.
- She's new to our class, but she knows a lot of English words.
- I'm sorry. There is nothing I can do, but I can show you a way to get out of this.
- I would do nothing but laugh.
- Everyone but him wants to go to the party.

#32, some

Pronounced səm

- Some students work hard.
- He made some money.
- Some countries are big.
- She visited some big countries.
- Some thirty students were in the trip.
- Listen to some music.
- Some of them.

- Although most countries are small, but some countries are big.
- Some students work after school to earn money.
- Some of them joined the trip to Europe.
- Some thirty students were in that trip.
- Some of them listen to music, and some of them listen to English lessons.

158

#33, what

Pronounced wät

- What time is it?
- What's your name?
- What?
- What we need to succeed is this.
- Do what you can.
- What does it mean?
- What do you mean?

- What time is it?
- It's nine o'clock.
- What's your name?
- My name is Wei Ke.
- What?
- Wei Ke.
- What does it mean?
- It means a great scientist in Chinese.
- What a wonderful name!
- Thanks.
- What we need to succeed is set a goal, take action, and keep working on it until we succeed.

#34, there

Pronounced THer

- Stay there.
- Over there.
- There she is.
- Hi there!
- There's a supermarket next to it.
- There are almost 200 countries in the world.
- There are 7000 languages in the world.

- Where is Victor?
- He's over there.
- Where?
- Over at the T-Mobile store. There's a supermarket next to it.
- There he is!

#35, we

Pronounced we

- We are students.
- Shall we learn together?
- We'll learn together.
- What are we learning?
- We're learning English.

- We'll either find a way to succeed or make a way to succeed.
- If we don't find the things we're looking for, make them!
- If we don't pronounce these English words right, make us pronounce them right!

#36, can

Pronounced kan

- I can do it.
- I can speak English.
- We can help others.
- You can use it.
- Can you hear me?
- It can be done.

- Student: Can I go to the bathroom?
- Teacher: I don't know. Can you?
- Student: May I?
- Teacher: Yes. You may.

- What I can do is what I have the ability to do. What I will do is what I'll get my results from.
- Out of the 7.2 billion people in the world, 795 million are hungry.
- There are many ways we can help these hungry people.

#37, out

Pronounced out

- In or out?
- He's out.
- Out of nowhere.
- Out there.
- A way out.

- Do you want to stay in or stay out?
- Is Victor home? No he's out.
- Victor suddenly appears out of nowhere!
- There are many successful people out there whom you can learn from.
- We either find a way out or make a way out.

#38, other

Pronounced əTHər

- One or the other.
- Would you like this one or the other one?
- The other side of the page.
- Any other.

- Which one would you like? This one or the other one?
- The other one.
- You can use this one or the other one.
- Let's look at the other side of the page.
- Another way to learn to pronounce "other" is through video.
- Any other questions?

#39, were

Pronounced wər

Today → are
Yesterday → were

- There are 12 students here today.
- There were 11 students here yesterday.
- There were many opportunities.
- They were sitting right here.
- There were here until ten.
- You started when you were in preschool.
- Apples were $1 for three.

- There were many opportunities to raise my hands to ask questions in today's class.
- The teachers were sitting right here.
- They were here helping until ten.
- You were good friends when you were in preschool.
- Apple were $1 for three yesterday.

#40, all

Pronounced ôl

- Is that all?
- That's all.
- All of them.
- All I want for these six months is to learn to speak English fluently.
- That's not all we're going to learn today. We'll learn more.

- All of the students in this class came from different countries.
- All I want for these six months is to get rid of my accent and speak English like a native.
- World language is not all we're going to learn today. We'll learn something else.

It's time to learn the words in context again.

- My name is Victor.
- I came from Russia.
- There are almost 200 countries in the world.
- Although most countries are small, but some countries are big.
- Russia is the world's biggest country. The second biggest is Canada and the third biggest is America.
- Russia is about as big as Canada and America combined.
- All of the students in this class came from different countries.
- There are 7000 languages in the world, but world language wasn't all we've learned today.
- There were many opportunities to raise our hands to ask questions in today's class.
- The teachers were sitting right here.
- They were here helping until ten.
- Students were sitting right there.
- We asked questions until the teachers were gone.
- There are many successful people out there whom we can learn from.
- There are many ways we can succeed.
- If we can dream it, we can achieve it.

- You can use this one or the other one.
- Which one would you like? This one or the other one?
- The other one.
- What I can do is what I have the ability to do, but if I don't take action, nothing will happen. What I will do is what I'll focus on and take actions to do which will

167

get me results.
- Out of the 7.2 billion people in the world, 795 million are hungry.
- There are many ways we can help these hungry people.

If there are nine rabbits on the ground and you want to catch one, just focus on one.
Jack Ma

Chapter 8: 41 – 50, English-Speaking Countries

#41, your

Pronounced yôr

- – Your book.
- – Your name.
- – Your car.
- – What's your country of origin?
- – Is that your book?
- – The story will make your heart smile.

#42, when

Pronounced wen

- When was the test? It was yesterday.
- When I was a child, I went swimming in the river.
- When did you come to America?
- Today is when I'll get my things done.
- I wear a jacket when it's cold.

- When there are American, Australian, British and other accents to choose from, I choose American accent since I live in America.
- When you focus your attention on one thing, your energy will flow to it.

#43, up

Pronounced əp

- – Jumping up and down.
- – Get up in the morning.
- – The up escalator.
- – Sales were up last month.
- – What are you up to?

#44, use

Pronounced yo͞os

- Use a pen to write.
- Use a cup to drink.
- Use our mind to think.
- Used to be this way.
- The use of water.
- Water has many uses.

- Use our mind well and we'll succeed.
- Use Myfluentenglish Formula to speak English like a native in six months.
- Like other languages, the English language used to be a small language, but it's become a big language today.

#45, word

Pronounced wərd

- One word.
- Two words.
- An English word.
- A Spanish word.
- Learn a word a day.
- A man of his word.

- "Excellent" is an wonderful word.
- A good way to build a vocabulary is to listen to a word a day.
- My English teacher is a man of his words. He does whatever he says.

#46, how

Pronounced hou

- How have you been?
- How does it work?
- How did it go?
- How old are you?
- How nice!

- How nice it is to speak more than one language.
- How wonderful to see it happen!
- How did you like your trip to Europe? It was wonderful!

#47, said

Pronounced sed
Today → say
Yesterday → said

- He said, "Thank you."
- "It's OK," I said.
- The clock said one thirty.

- "What did she say when you asked her to go to your house?" She said, "No."
- Mr. Xiao said, "It's OK to make mistakes."
- He also said, "The more mistakes you make, the more you'll learn, and the more successful you'll be."

177

#48, an

Pronounced an

An = a.
An is used in front of a vowel (a, e, i, o, u).

- A word.
- An English word.
- A country.
- An European country.
- A British accent.
- An American accent.
- A seventeen-day vacation.
- An eighteen-day vacation.

#49, each

Pronounced ēCH

- – Each day.
- – Each book.
- – Each one.
- – Each and everyone of us.
- – Twenty-five cents each.

- – Apples are 25 cents each.
- – Each of us gets a textbook.

#50, she

Pronounced SHē

- A boy is a he. A girl is a she.
- Is that a he or a she?
- It's a she.
- She wants to learn English.

- Claire came from Argentina.
- She wants to learn to speak English like a native speaker.
- "Hello. May I speak to Claire, please?" "This is she."

Let's use these 10 words.

- Hi! My name is Claire.
- Many people ask me where I was from by saying "Where are you from?"
- One person asked me this way, "What's your country of origin?"
- One person asked, "Where did you come from?"
- I came from Argentina.
- I came to America two years ago.
- Something I learned in my English class made my eyes open.

- The English language used to be a small language, but it has become a big language today.
- Three major accents presently exist: The American accent with 250 million speakers, the British accent with 60 million speakers, and the Australian accent with 17 million speakers.

- I'm learning American accent.
- A good way to build a vocabulary is to learn a word a day.
- My English teacher is a man of his words. He does what he says.
- He said, "Use your mind well and you'll succeed."
- How nice it is to speak more than one language.

Always remember, your focus determines your reality.
George Lucas

Chapter 9: 51 – 60, Types Of English

#51, which

Pronounced wiCH

- Which one?
- Which language?
- Which accent?

- Which one is your book?
- There are two books there. Which one is yours?
- There are several major English accents to learn. Which accent is your choice?

#52, do

Pronounced doo

- I do my homework every day.
- Do your best.
- What do you do?
- Do you have any brothers and sisters?
- Which accent do you choose?

#53, their

Pronounced THer

- Their language.
- Their accent.
- Their book.
- Their children.
- Their friends.

- European immigrants brought their languages to America.
- They also brought their accents which contributed to the American English accent.
- Their children quickly learn the new language.

#54, time

Pronounced tīm

- What time is it?
- It's eight o'clock.
- What's the time?
- It's ten thirty.
- It's time to go home.

#55, if

Pronounced if

- If it rains, we'll bring an umbrella.
- If we use it, we'll keep it.
- If this, then that.
- If you do your homework, then you'll pass the test.

- If I set my goal, take action, and keep working on it, I will succeed.
- If you persevere, then you will succeed.

#56, will

Pronounced wil

- Accents will change.
- You will be OK.
- Will you be here?

- Will you teach me how to say this word? Sure.
- You will succeed if you'd keep working on it.
- If you have faith, you will persevere.

#57, way

Pronounced wā

- One way.
- Way to go.
- Make a way.
- There's a way out.

- One way to learn English is to repeat what you hear again and again.
- If we can't find a way, make a way.

#58, about

Pronounced ə'bout

- These apples are about five pounds.
- There are about 20 trees in the garden.
- What are you talking about?
- I was thinking about learning American English.
- This book is about how to speak English.

#58, many

Pronounced menē

- How many brothers and sisters do you have?
- Many students speak more than one language at home.
- Many people learn American English.
- Immigrants brought many European accents to America.
- We make many mistakes in life, but we learn many lessons from our mistakes.

#60, then

Pronounced THen

- I set my goal and then achieved my goal.
- The teacher came and then the students came.
- She first learned British accent and then American accent.
- If you study for the test, then you'll pass the test.
- If you do your homework, then you'll be OK.
- Let's meet at noon. See you then.

It's that time again. Let's put these words in context.

- There are three major English accents. Which one are you learning?
- For me. I'm learning American accent.
- My name is Aadhya.
- I was born in India and immigrated to the United States with my parents.
- Like the early European immigrants who brought their accents to America, I brought my accent, too.
- I first learned British English when I was in India, then I started to learn American English after I came to America.
- My English teacher said, "A good way to learn to speak English is to repeat what you hear again and again."
- I find it very useful.
- After I repeat what I hear again and again, new English words are keep building in my subconscious mind.
- If I set my goal, take action, and keep working on it, I will succeed.
- When I face obstacles, I often think about giving up. If I have faith, I will never give up.
- Even if I make many mistakes, but if I persevere, I will be closer and closer to my destination.

- What time is it?
- It's eight thirty.
- What's the time now?
- It's half pass eight.
- It's time to go home.
- Many students speak more than one language at

home. I'm one of them.

Decide what you want and believe you can get it.
Anthony Robbins

Chapter 10: 61 – 70, American English

#61, them

Pronounced T̲Hem

I → me
You → you
He → him
She → her
We → us
They → them

- They learn English with us.
- We learn English with them.
- Do you know them? No. Let's talk to them.
- Let's perfect these words and say them right.

- They're good students. One of them is their team captain.
- If we hangout with them, we'll be good students, too.

#62, would

Pronounced wo͝od

- Would you like some gum?
- Would you like one?
- Yes, I would love to have one.
- How nice would it be to learn to speak English like a native.
- The weather would be nice for a while.
- I would visit Arizona and Wyoming if I got two weeks off.
- If I were you, I would live in the west coast.
- If I have one more day, I will go to Yellowstone.
- If I had one more day, I would go to Yellowstone.
- Would you repeat the last sentence, please?

#63, write

Pronounced rīt

- Write a letter.
- Write an email.
- Write to a friend.
- Write on a map.
- Write down your goal.

- Set our goal and write it down.
- Why do we write down our goals?
- Those who write down their goals accomplish significantly more than those who don't write down their goals.

#64, like

Pronounced līk

- I like the warm weather of the west coast.
- They like to Tango.
- Would you like to Tango?
- You speak like a native.
- Living in Seattle makes me feel like living in nature.

- Would you like to Tango? Yes, I would like to.
- Would you like to Tango? Yes, I would love to.

#65, so

Pronounced sō

- Do you think so?
- I think so.
- The temperature in eastern Canada is so cold in the winter.
- The temperature in western Canada is so warm in the winter.
- The equator is so hot and so is Phoenix.
- It was so hot in Phoenix, so I moved to Seattle.
- It's so effective to repeat what you hear again and again, so I'm using it.
- My pronunciation is improving so quickly, so I'm going to continue practicing.

#66, these

Pronounced THēz
One → this
Two or more → these

- This book.
- These books.
- This is.
- These are.
- Is this your book?
- Are these your books?

- These cities are hot in the summer.
- These states are cold in the winter.
- These words are useful in daily English.

#67, her

Pronounced hər

I → me
He → him
She → her

I → my
He → his
She → her

- Do you know her?
- She knows you like her.
- This is her book.
- She always brings her phone with her.

#68, long

Pronounced lôNG

- It's been a long time.
- She has long hair.
- Canada has long days in the summer.
- Canada has long nights in the winter.
- The Mississippi River is 2,202 miles long.

- The longest river in the US is the Missouri River. It's 2,341 miles long.
- When waiting in a long line, it's a great time to listen to an audio book.

#69, make

Pronounced māk

- Make lunch.
- Make friends.
- Make money.
- Make a living.
- Make it on time.

- We'll make it on time.
- It's easy to make a living in America.
- You'll make some new friends in your first day of school.

#70, thing

Pronounced THiNG

- One thing.
- One more thing.
- One thing to consider.

- That is one thing to think about.
- The other thing is the weather.
- One more thing to think about is the time zone.

You know it's coming. Let's learn these words in context.

- If you were to drive from New York to Seattle without stopping, it would take you two days.
- The temperature in eastern Canada is so cold in the winter.
- The temperature in western Canada is so warm in the winter.
- Canada has long days in the summer.
- Canada has long nights in the winter.
- The equator is so hot and so is Phoenix City.
- It was so hot in Phoenix, so I moved to Seattle.
- I would visit Arizona, Wyoming and Utah if I get two weeks off.
- These states are cold in the winter and hot in the summer.
- I like the warm weather of the west coast.
- My name is Mei. I came from China.
- I have visited 40 of the 50 states in America and part of Canada.
- North America is an amazing place to live.
- It's easy to make a living in America.
- One thing to think about is the weather.
- Another thing to think about is the time zone.

- This is a world map.
- These are state maps.
- The longest river in the US is the Missouri River.
- The Missouri River flows from Montana through North Dakota, South Dakota, Nebraska, Kansas, Iowa, and Missouri.
- It's 2,341 miles long.
- Let's write on the state maps to plan our trip.

209

- Do you know her?
- Yes. She's a successful person. She's the president of the Success Impact Group.
- The Success Impact Group?
- Yes. Everyone is that group is a successful person.
- If we become friends with them, we'll be successful, too.
- This is her book. She published it last year.
- She always listens to audio books on her phone even when she has only a moment to spare.
- She said, "When waiting in a long line, it's a great time to listen to an audio book."
- She always sets her goals and writes them down.
- I asked her why bother to write down our goals?
- She said, "Those who write down their goals accomplish significantly more than those who don't write down their goals."
- She's a successful person. I'm going to learn form her.

Energy flows where attention goes.
Hawaiian Proverb

Chapter 11: 71 – 80, North America Climates

#71, see

Pronounced sē

- I see a frozen lake.
- They come to see a friend.
- Want to see how it works?

- If you go to Lake Michigan in the winter, you'll see a frozen lake.
- If you go to Yellowstone National Park, you'll see geysers shooting out hot water.
- Do you want to see how it works? Sure.

#72, him

Pronounced him
I → me
She → her
He → him

- Do you know him?
- Can you give this to him?
- Would you like to ask him to come with us?
- He knows she likes him.

- In California's Death Valley, summer is hot for him.
- California's mild winter is just right for him.

#73, two

Pronounced to̅o

- One and one is two.
- Two and four is six.
- Two times two is four.
- Two of my friends.

- The U.S. and Canada are two friendly countries in north America.
- I'll build my wealth with my own two hands.

#74, has

Pronounced haz

He → has
She → has
It → has
I, you, they → have

- Virginia has four seasons.
- Hawaii has one season.
- Alaska has a long and dark winter.
- Northern Canada has a long and bright summer.
- He's got two children → He has got two children → He has two children.
- She's got a teacher's certificate → She has a teacher's certificate.
- It has to be that way.

#75, look

Pronounced lŏok

- Look at.
- Do you want to look at it?
- Look for.
- What are you looking for?
- You look great!
- Take a look!

- We can look through the clouds to see the stars.
- If you look around Seattle, you'll see lots of hiking trails.
- With 360 sunny days a year, I look at life differently in New Mexico.
- If you look for a warm place to live, go to California.
- Look at Mt. Denali. It's the highest mountain peak in north America.
- Look at the midnight sun! Welcome to Alaska!

#76, more

Pronounced môr

- Would you like some more?
- Do you want some more?
- Want some more?
- If I have one more day, I will go to Yellowstone.
- There are more people in California than in any other state.
- Persistence is more important than talent.
- I like Seattle's cool summer days more than Houston's hot summer days.
- I'll be more than happy to help you.

#77, day

Pronounced dā

- There are 24 hours a day.
- There are seven days a week.
- There are 30 days a month.
- There are 365 days a year.
- An average person needs to sleep eight hours a day.

- We work for eight hours day and sleep for eight hours a day. What we do with the remaining eight hours determines what we'll achieve.

#78, could

Pronounced kŏŏd

Present → can
Past → could

- They could be right.
- That could be the right answer.
- Could I use the phone?
- Could you be more precise?

#79, go

Pronounced gō

- Go to a meeting.
- Go to school.
- Let's go to Toronto.
- I must go now.
- Let's give it a go to see what it'll do.

#80, come

Pronounced kəm

- Come to America.
- Come to my house.
- Come to the library.
- Easy come, easy go.
- Tomorrow has not yet to come.
- We come in peace.
- Your lunch comes with soup.
- Your dinner comes with salad.

It's time to learn these words in context.

- Winter is so cold in Michigan.
- If you come to Lake Michigan in the winter, you'll see a frozen lake.
- Summer is so hot in Arizona.
- He comes to Arizona to see a friend.
- Summer is too hot for them.
- The U.S. and Canada are two friendly countries in north America.
- The U.S. mainland has four seasons while Hawaii has one.
- Alaska has a long and dark winter while northern Canada has a long and bright summer. If you look up at midnight, you can see the sun still up in the sky.
- In 360 sunny days a year, you don't need look through the clouds to see the stars in New Mexico.
- If you look for a warm place to live, go to California.
- If you look around Seattle, you'll see lots of hiking trails in the city and in the surrounding areas.
- I like Seattle's cool summer days more than Houston's hot summer days.
- If I had one more day, I would go to Yellowstone.
- There are more people in California than in any other state.

- There are 24 hours a day.
- An average person sleeps eight hours a day and works eight hours day. What he or she does with the remaining eight hours determines what he or she will achieve in life.
- Persistence is more important than talent. If you work on an area two hours a day for 20 years, you'll

223

be the best in the world in that area.
- It has been that way.
- That could be the answer you've been looking for in learning English.
- Let's give it a go and see what will happen.

Keep your focus laser-locked on what you want to create in your life.
Mike Basevic

Chapter 12: 81 – 90, 10 Largest Cities In The U.S. And Canada

#81, did

Pronounced did

Today → do
Yesterday → did

- Did you see that? Yes. I did.
- He did a good job.
- How long did it take you?
- They did it in three hours.
- What did you do?
- She did my hair last week.

- Why did you choose New York?
- Because New York is the largest city in America.
- I did 35 miles per hour in New York City and got pulled over by a cop.
- What's the speed limit in New York City? 30.
- When he was driving in New York, he made every right turn on red light.
- Did he get pulled over by the police? Yes. He did.

#82, my

Pronounced mī

- My name is _____.
- My English is improving every day.
- My city is Los Angeles.

- My goodness. My city is the second biggest city in America.

#83, sound

Pronounced sound

- Sound wave.
- Listen to the sound of your heart.
- The sound of a subway train.
- The sound of your voice.
- Sound the alarm.
- How does that sound?
- That sounds like a plan.

- You had an exciting adventure in Toronto by the sound of your voice.
- With a population of 2.8 million, Toronto sounds like a big city.
- Yes, indeed. Toronto is the biggest city in Canada and the third biggest in north America after New York and Los Angeles.

#84, no

Pronounced nō

- No Smoking.
- Is there anything wrong? No. Everything is fine.
- Are you a teacher? No. I'm a student.
- Is this your book? No. It's his.
- There is no need.
- This is no easy job.
- I'll be back in no time.

- There is no need to bring a jacket. Unlike San Francisco, Chicago's summer is not cold.
- Swimming across the Great Lakes is no easy task, but I'll be back in no time.

#85, most

Pronounced mōst

- The most populous city.
- The most important day in my life.
- Most of everyone agreed.
- Most of the world is made of water.

- Houston is the most populous city in Texas and the fifth most populous city in north America.
- The most important day in my life is the day I discovered the formula to success.
- Most of everyone agreed that education is the most important factor to success except for me. I disagreed with that.
- Thomas Edison, one of the most famous inventors who invented the electric light bulb, had only three months of formal education.
- According to Professor Duckworth, the most important factor to success is to keep working on it.

#86, number

Pronounced nembər

- Number one.
- Number two.
- What's your phone number?
- The number of residents of Montreal is numbered more than 1.7 million.
- The number of visitors.
- Tourists Increase the number of jobs.

- The number of visitors to Montreal is more than 10 times of its population.
- The number of tourists to Montreal increases the number of jobs.
- Montreal is the number six largest city in north America and the number two best city to live in the world.

#87, who

Pronounced hoo

- Who's that?
- Who are you?
- Who's the major of Philadelphia?

- Who wants to go to Philadelphia to see the liberty bell?
- Who wants to guess what the seventh largest city in north America is?

#88, over

Pronounced ōvər

- Over there.
- Over here.
- The White House is over in Washington DC.
- Phoenix is over in Arizona.
- There is rarely any clouds over Phoenix.
- Dobbins Lookout is a great place to look over Phoenix.
- Over in Dobbins is a great lookout.
- She speaks over a loudspeaker.

- I would choose to stay in Seattle over Phoenix in the summer.
- The Phoenix summer temperature is over 105 degrees.
- The Superbowl game in Phoenix is over.

#89, know

Pronounced nō

- I know.
- Do you know?

- Do you know him? Yes. I know him.
- Do you know what San Antonio means? No, but I know it's the name of a city.
- I know what the ninth largest city in north America is. It's San Antonio, Texas.
- Do you know the population of San Antonio? Yes. It's 1.5 million.

#90, water

Pronounced wôdər

- A glass of water.
- Hot water.
- Cold water.
- Surrounded by water.

- Most of our body is water.
- San Diego is a city next to water.
- Let's water the plants.
- They added water to their juice.
- Would you like some water?
- In San Diego, you get 10 inches of rain a year. Be sure to water your plants well.

You know it well. It's time to use the words again.

- Why did you choose to live in New York City?
- Because New York City is the largest city in America.
- A friend visited me last week.
- While he was driving in New York, he made right turns on red light and got pulled over by the police. He didn't know why he was pulled over.
- What did the police say?
- The police said no turn on red in New York City.
- Did he get a ticket?
- No. He was lucky that he didn't get a ticket.
- Where does he live?
- He lives in Los Angeles.
- Is it legal to turn right on red in Los Angeles?
- Yes. It's legal to turn right on red in all cities in America except for New York City. New York City is the only city in America where right turn on red light is illegal.
- My goodness. With a population of 8.6 million, it must be because New York City is so crowded.
- Being the second largest city in America, Los Angeles has a much smaller population.
- Los Angeles has two subway lines and four light rail lines.
- Do not use the emergency brakes as handles while riding on the train. It'll sound the alarm and the operator will stop the train immediately.

- You had an exciting adventure in Toronto by the sound of your voice.
- With a population of 2.8 million, Toronto sounds like a big city.

237

- Yes, indeed. Toronto is the biggest city in Canada and the third biggest in north America after New York and Los Angeles.
- Is anything wrong for being the biggest in Canada? No, everything is fine.
- In fact, there is no need to worry about safety in Toronto because Toronto is one of the safest cities in North America.
- There is no need to bring a jacket. Unlike San Francisco, Chicago's summer is not cold.
- It's no easy task to swim across the Great Lakes, but I'll be back in no time.

- Houston is the largest city in Texas and the fifth largest in north America.
- Montreal is the number six largest city in north America and the number two best city to live in the world.
- The number of residents of Montreal is numbered more than 1.7 million.
- The number of visitors to Montreal is more than 10 times of its population.
- The number of tourists to Montreal increases the number of jobs.
- Who's that?
- That's the major of Philadelphia?
- Who wants to go to Philadelphia to see the liberty bell?
- I'm in!
- Who wants to guess what the seventh largest city in north America is?
- It's Philadelphia.
- Phoenix is over in Arizona. With mostly sunny days

year round, there is rarely any clouds over Phoenix.
- With the summer temperature of over 105 degrees, I would choose to stay in San Francisco over Phoenix in the summer.

- Do you know what San Antonio means? No, but I know it's the name of a city.
- I know what the ninth largest city in north America is. It's San Antonio, Texas.
- Do you know the population of San Antonio? Yes. It's 1.5 million.
- Do you know him? Yes. I know him well. He's a good friend of mine and the major of San Antonio. He has a good habit.
- What is it?
- He likes to drink lots of water.
- That's a wonderful thing. An average person needs to drink eight glasses of water a day.
- Do you shower in hot water or cold water? Cold water because it's hot in San Diego.
- In San Diego, the tenth largest city in north America, you get 10 inches of rain a year. Be sure to water your plants well.

Whatever the mind can conceive and believe
it can achieve.
Napoleon Hill

Chapter 13: 91 – 100, U.S. And Canada Culture

#91, than

Pronounced THən

- Two is bigger than one.
- Five is more than two.
- A meter is longer than a foot.

- Canada is a little bit bigger than America.
- America has a much bigger population than Canada.
- American has nine times more people than Canada has.
- A gallon is heavier than a liter.

#92, call

Pronounced kôl

- – A telephone call.
- – I'll give you a call tonight.
- – I'll call you tonight.
- – I'll give you a ring tonight (I'll give you a call tonight).
- – Who made that phone call?
- – Let's wrap it up and call it a day.
- – My name is Yoon-Jin. My friends called me Jack.
- – They called their daughter Katie.
- – The US is called a melting pot.

#93, first

Pronounced fərst

- First day at school.
- First job in Canada.
- First apartment I lived.
- Let's eat first and then go to the movie.
- First grade.
- First time.
- The first to get here will be the winner.

- What grade is your child in? My child is in first grade.
- Have you seen snow before? No. This is my first time seeing snow.

#94, people

Pronounced ˈpēpəl

One → person
Two or more → people

- How many people are there in your class?
- My people live in Montana.
- I've had my people working on this project for a while now.

- How many people signed up for the trip to Europe?
- Forty-six people.
- There are 7.2 billion people in the world. Five hundred and twenty-seven million people speak English.
- When looking at a photo, what do you look at first? The people or the background?
- I always look at the people first.

#95, may

Pronounced mā

- May I use your pen? Yes. You may.
- My I borrow your eraser? Sure! You may.
- That may be true.
- It may be easy for you.
- The month of May.

- May I use your pen? Sure.
- *Think and Grow Rich* may have been an old book, but it has been the bestselling book in personal achievement.
- Learning to speak English may be easy for you.
- It may be easier than you thought.
- I was born in the month of May.

#96, down

Pronounced doun

- Sit down, please.
- He climbed down the mountain.
- He fell down from the tree.
- Keep the noise down.
- The elevator is going down.
- The down escalator.
- My computer was down yesterday.
- Write down your goal.
- A $1000 down payment.
- Walk down the street.

- To buy a car in the U.S., you only need to put down a $1000 down payment, and the car will be ready for you to pick up the next day.
- When you're in the library, keep your voice down.
- Writing down your goal will keep you focusing on it.

#97, side

Pronounced sīd

- On one side of the page.
- On the other side of the road.
- Stand on my side.
- A side order.
- A side dish.
- Both sides agreed to sign a contract.

- No matter what decisions I make, my family always stands on my side.
- Having a supportive family on my side accelerates my success.
- In England, you drive on the left side of the road, but in America, you drive on the right side.
- I'd like a house salad with the dressing on the side, please.
- The two sides agreed to start trading.

#98, been

Pronounced bin

- How long have you been in the U.S.?
- How long have your been living in Canada?
- I have been learning English for three years.
- Where have you been?
- How have been doing for the past three years?
- It has been a wonderful trip.
- Have you been here before?

- How long have you been to the U.S.? Three years.
- How long have your been living in Canada? Two years.
- Your English is good! How long have been learning?
- I've been learning for three years.
- Where have you been lately? I have been visiting a friend in Canada.
- How have been doing for the past three years? I have perfected my English!
- It has been a wonderful trip to Canada!
- Have you been there before? Yes. I've been there three times.

#99, now

Pronounced nou

- If I start to practice my English now, I'll be speaking like a native six months from now.
- Now it's time to begin.
- I've been working here for three months now.
- It's been done. Now what?
- Now let's relax.

#100, find

Pronounced fīnd

- Do you want to find a warm place to live?
- Did you find the key?
- We need to find our way home.
- I turned around to find her smiling.

- We're on earth to find what we want. If we don't find what we want, make what we want!

Congratulations! This the last set of ten.

- I'm Don.
- I'm Harry.
- Please to meet you.
- Please to meet you.
- How long have you been to the U.S.?
- Three years. How long have your been living in Canada?
- Two years.
- Your English is good!
- Thanks. I have been learning English for three years.
- Waitress: "May I take your order?"
- Yes, please. I'll take a veggie sandwich and a house salad with the dressing on the side, please."
- Waitress: "Certainly."
- I'll take a chicken sandwich and a side order of French fries, please.
- Waitress: "Anything else?"
- That'll be all.

- Canada is little bit bigger than America, but America has a much bigger population than Canada.
- American has nine times more people than Canada has.
- Both America and Canada welcome immigrants from around the world, but America is called a cultural melting pot while Canada is called a cultural mosaic.
- There are 7.2 billion people in the world. Five hundred and twenty-seven million people speak English. Most of them live in north America.
- One of the most influential people in north America is Napoleon Hill.

- His book, *Think and Grow Rich*, may have been an old book, but it has been the bestselling book in personal achievement.
- One of the strategies in Hill's book is to write down your goal.
- Using the step-by-step instructions in this book, learning to speak English may be easier than you thought.
- If I start to practice my English now, I'll be speaking like a native six months from now.
- Now it's time to begin.
- Having a supportive family on my side accelerates my success.
- No matter what decisions I make, my family always stands on my side.
- We come to earth to find what we want. If we don't find what we want, we make what we want!
- Congratulations on getting this far. Let's wrap it up and call it a lesson.

Keep practicing and you *will* speak like a native!

Inspired? Leave a review on Amazon for two reasons.

1. Readers do take your review seriously!
2. You'll receive a PDF edition of this book (a $37 value) for free. Just send an email to ken@myfluentenglish.com after you left your review.

Made in the USA
San Bernardino, CA
18 March 2017